PAT CHAPMAN

North Indian Curries

PAT CHAPMAN

North Indian Curries

Photography by Simon Wheeler

WEIDENFELD & NICOLSON

Pat Chapman

Pat Chapman's passion for curry was virtually inherited, his ancestors having been in India for 200 years.

He founded the world-renowned Curry Club in 1982, and it was not long before he set up a national network of curry restaurant reporters, which led to his regular publishing of the highly successful *Good Curry Restaurant Guide*, with its prestigious awards to top restaurants.

Pat frequently broadcasts on television and radio, and holds regular cookery courses. He is often to be seen demonstrating at major food shows and stores.
He is a consultant chef to a number of UK Indian restaurants and he has appeared as a guest chef for Hilton Hotels, Club Med France and Selfridges Restaurant in London, as well as at Bombay's celebrated Taj Mahal Intercontinental hotel.

Pat is best known as a cookery author. His 20 books have sold more than
1 million copies, and include such best sellers as *The Curry Club 250 Favourite Curries and Accompaniments*, *The Balti Curry Cookbook*, *Curry Club Indian Restaurant Cookbook*, *Quick and Easy Curries* for BBC Books and *Curries* in the Master Chefs series by Orion. His repertoire also includes book on Thai, Chinese, Bangladeshi and Middle Eastern cooking.

Contents

Think of northern India and you think
Moghul. Think Moghul and you're
thinking of the Taj Mahal.
This wonder of the world, built as
a memorial to an emperor's wife,
epitomizes Moghulai superlatives.
Another legacy of those heady days, and
a wonder of the culinary world, is
classic north Indian Moghulai cuisine.

Introduction

India's most fabulous dynasty began at the time of the English Tudors, and remained all-powerful for some 200 years, in the hands of just six emperors, known as the Great Moghuls. Everything they did was magnificent. Their army consisted of 100,000 heavily armed men, 10,000 camels, 5,000 cannon and 1,000 war elephants, and was invincible. Their rule, though austere for their subjects, created great wealth and a luxurious lifestyle for themselves. Opulence at court was displayed in exaggerated robes, oversized jewels, huge harems of 1,000 women and their eunuch guards, elephant jousting, massive parades, ostentatious parties. Their four great cities of Srinagar, Lahore, Delhi and Agra were unparalleled in their forts, palaces, gardens, mosques and mausoleums – as is witnessed Agra's Taj Mahal, built by Emperor Shah Jehan as a memorial to his wife Mumtaz after her premature death.

Food did not escape Moghul attention. Northern Indian cuisine had been evolving for thousands of years, but Moghulai chefs took it to the heights of perfection, matching the savouriness of the Punjab with the aromatics of Kashmir, while creating a creamy delicacy which remains, to this day, distinctly Moghul. Great banquets were frequently held at court, and no one was more important than the emperor's personal chef. It is said that the Emperor Akbar's inner court was composed of just nine advisors, known as the Navrattan, of which the chef was one, along with the prime minister, senior general, physician, astrologer, musician, poet, artist and biographer. True or not, Moghulai cooking has not been bettered since those days, and it is the backbone of all cooking in the modern Indian restaurant.

Here are twelve of the best classical North Indian Moghulai recipes. Their ingredients and spices are widely available, and I've 'modernized' them so that they are easy to prepare and cook. I sincerely hope you will enjoy their subtle, aromatic spicing, and that these twelve recipes will become as much your favourites as they are mine.

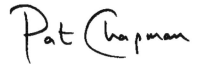

Maharajah sheek kebab
Mince kebabs

SERVES 4 AS A STARTER

600 g/1¼ lb lean beef, lamb,
   pork or venison, or skinless
   chicken, turkey or duck breast
4–6 garlic cloves, chopped
2 tablespoons dried onion flakes
   (page 35)
1 tablespoon garam masala
   (page 37)
2 teaspoons bottled mild curry
   paste
1–3 fresh green chillies, seeded
   and chopped (optional)
2 tablespoons chopped fresh
   coriander leaves
1 tablespoon chopped fresh mint
   leaves
1 teaspoon salt

Preheat the oven to 190°C/375°F/Gas Mark 5.

Chop the meat into cubes, removing all fat and gristle. Place the meat and all the other ingredients in a food processor and pulse-grind until the mixture becomes relatively smooth.

Divide the mixture into four large or eight small pieces, then shape each piece into a sausage. If you wish, form the sausage shapes on skewers.

Place on a baking sheet and bake for 10–12 minutes. Serve hot or cold.

Serve with fresh, crisp baguettes, lime wedges and a salad of shredded spinach, rocket, radicchio, spring onion and celeriac, tossed with a dressing of 4 tablespoons olive oil mixed with 6 tablespoons Greek-style yogurt and ½ teaspoon each of chilli and mango powder, with some chopped garlic and fresh chives.

SHALIMAR RAAN
Spicy roast leg of lamb

SERVES 4 – 6 AS A STARTER

1.5–1.6 kg /3–3½ lb leg of
lamb, on the bone
450–500g /about 1 lb Greek-
style yogurt
4 tablespoons vegetable oil
2 tablespoons garam masala
(page 37)
1 teaspoon ground cinnamon
1 teaspoon ground cloves
1 tablespoon bottled tandoori
paste
1–3 fresh red chillies
50 g/2 oz bottled beetroot
2 tablespoons chopped fresh
mint leaves
2 tablespoons chopped fresh
coriander leaves
1 teaspoon salt

Preheat the oven to 180°C/350°F/Gas Mark 4.

Trim all the fat and membranes off the leg of lamb,
then make a number of small gashes in the flesh. Put all
the remaining ingredients in a food processor and grind
to a paste.

Line a roasting tin with foil. Put the lamb in the tin and
coat it liberally all over with the spicy paste, using about
half the mixture. Loosely cover the lamb with more foil
and roast in the centre of the oven for about 2 hours.

Spread the lamb with about half the remaining spice
paste and roast (without the foil) for at least a further
hour. The flesh should fall off the bone, so it may need
more time to achieve this.

Remove the lamb from the oven and let it rest in a
warm place for about 15 minutes, during which time
you can make the gravy. Put the remaining spice paste
in a saucepan and add any cooked paste from the
roasting tin, together with a little water, salt and garam
masala. Simmer for about 3 minutes. Carve the lamb,
pour the gravy over it and serve hot.

*Traditionally, raan would be served with naan bread, liberally
spread with ghee. For a change, try it with roast potatoes and
light vegetables such as mangetout, courgette and celery, lightly
sautéed with butter, wild onion seeds (kalonji) and some cream.
Garnish with chilli powder and chopped chives. Cold raan
with pickle makes a great sandwich filler.*

SHAH JEHANI KORMA
Classic mild lamb curry

SERVES 4

675 g/1½ lb lean lamb, cubed
2 teaspoons sugar
1 teaspoon salt
250 ml/8 fl oz natural yogurt
4 tablespoons ghee or vegetable
   oil
½ teaspoon turmeric
2 teaspoons ground coriander
2 tablespoons finely chopped
   garlic
1 tablespoon finely chopped
   fresh ginger
2 onions, finely chopped
20–30 saffron strands
4 tablespoons ground almonds
175 ml/6 fl oz single cream

Whole spices
15 cm/6 inch piece of cassia
   bark
12 green cardamom pods
10 cloves
8 bay leaves
1 teaspoon fennel seeds

Garnish
toasted flaked almonds
fresh coriander leaves

Place the meat in a non-metallic bowl, add the whole spices, sugar, salt and yogurt, mix well and leave in the refrigerator to marinate for between 6 and 48 hours.

Preheat the oven to 190°C/375°F/Gas Mark 5.

Heat the ghee or oil in a wok or karahi, then carry out the initial fry (page 36) with the turmeric, coriander, garlic, ginger and onions.

Place the lamb and its marinade in a casserole, add the fried onion and spice mixture, stir well and place in the oven for 25 minutes.

Stir in the saffron, ground almonds and cream and return to the oven.

After 20 minutes, stir the curry and add a little water if it looks dry. Cook for a further 10–20 minutes, or until the lamb is very tender.

Serve at once, or cool, chill and reheat the next day. Garnish with toasted almonds and fresh coriander.

Accompany with either plain basmati rice or Navrattan pullao (page 28), and with the Potatoes in a pickle sauce (page 24) and the Queen's lentils (page 26), to make a Moghulai feast for 6–8 people.

DELHI SAG MIRCHI MURG
Chilli chicken with spinach

SERVES 4

675g/1½ lb skinless, boneless
  chicken breast
400g/14 oz young fresh spinach
  leaves
3 tablespoons vegetable oil
½ teaspoon turmeric
½ teaspoon chilli powder
1 teaspoon white cumin seeds
1 teaspoon ground cumin
4–6 garlic cloves, finely chopped
4–6 spring onions, chopped
125 ml/4 fl oz fragrant stock
  (page 37) or water
1 tablespoon tomato purée
1–3 fresh red chillies, seeded
  and cut into strips
2 teaspoons garam masala
  (page 37)
4 tablespoons chopped fresh
  coriander leaves
salt

Cut the chicken into bite-sized pieces.

Wash the spinach thoroughly and cut it into large bite-sized pieces.

Heat the oil in a wok. Add the turmeric, chilli powder and cumin, and stir-fry briskly for 20 seconds. Add 2–3 tablespoons water and stir well, then add the garlic and spring onions and stir-fry for about 2 minutes.

Add the stock or more water and stir in the tomato purée. As soon as the liquid begins to simmer, add the chicken pieces and the fresh chilli. Simmer for 5 minutes, stirring occasionally.

Add half the spinach, and stir it in gently. When it wilts, add the remaining spinach and stir briefly. Lower the heat, and simmer gently for about 5 minutes.

Add the garam masala, coriander and salt to taste. Stir-fry for a final minute, or until the chicken is cooked right through, then serve immediately.

Since this is so quick to cook, it makes a good light lunch or TV supper with plain rice or naan or pitta bread, which you can simply heat in the toaster.

AGRA HARSHA PASANDA
Creamy duck curry

SERVES 4

600 g/1¼ lb duck breast,
    fat removed
3 tablespoons vegetable oil
1 teaspoon fennel seeds
4–6 garlic cloves, finely chopped
2.5 cm/1 inch cube of fresh
    ginger, finely chopped
1 large onion, finely chopped
1 fennel bulb, finely chopped
400 ml/14 fl oz crème fraîche
2 tablespoons chopped fresh
    coriander leaves
1 teaspoon garam masala
salt

Marinade
100 ml/3 ½ fl oz red wine
2 tablespoons ground fennel
    seeds
2 tablespoons ground coriander
1 tablespoon brown sugar
½ teaspoon chilli powder
½ teaspoon salt

Cut the duck breast into slices about 8 mm/⅓ inch thick. Beat the slices with a rolling pin or the side of a cleaver until they form escalopes about 4 mm/¹⁄₁₆ inch thick. Place in a shallow, non-metallic bowl. Mix the marinade ingredients together and pour over the duck escalopes. Cover and refrigerate for a minimum of 1 hour, up to a maximum of 24 hours.

To cook, preheat the oven to 190°C/375°F/Gas Mark 5.

Heat the oil in a wok or karahi, then carry out the initial fry (page 36) with the fennel seeds, garlic, ginger and onion.

Transfer the caramelized onion mixture to a lidded casserole dish, add the duck with its marinade, and place in the oven.

After 20 minutes, stir in the fennel and cream and return to the oven.

After a further 20 minutes, stir in the coriander, garam masala and salt to taste. Return to the oven for a final 20–30 minutes, until the duck is tender. If the dish looks dry during the cooking, stir in a little water. Serve hot.

Superb with rice and curried vegetables, or try it in an unconventional way, with creamed mashed potatoes and asparagus tips.

KASHMIRI MACHLI
Aromatic fish curry

**SERVES 4 AS A MAIN COURSE,
8 AS A STARTER**

4 fresh mackerel, about
 325 g/12 oz each, scaled
 and gutted

Marinade
225 g/8 oz Greek-style yogurt
1 large onion, chopped
8 garlic cloves, quartered
5 cm/2 inch cube of fresh ginger,
 chopped
1–4 fresh green chillies, seeded
 and chopped
30–40 fresh sweet basil leaves
1 tablespoon tomato purée
1 tablespoon garam masala
1 teaspoon salt

Wash the fish inside and out and pat dry. Make a few gashes in the flesh with the tip of a sharp knife.

Put all the marinade ingredients in a food processor and grind, adding enough water to make a thickish paste. Put the fish in a shallow, non-metallic dish, coat each fish with the marinade, cover and refrigerate for a minimum of 1 hour, up to a maximum of 4 hours.

To cook, preheat the grill to medium. Place the fish on the grill rack and grill for about 8 minutes. Turn and grill for a further 5–6 minutes. Serve hot.

To me this is a summertime barbecue dish, so why not serve it with a baked potato with soured cream, dusted with garam masala? Savour the fish with a glass of chilled dry rosé wine. A half portion makes a great starter, served with slices of buttered brown bread, a green salad and lemon wedges.

Punjabi methi jingri
Fenugreek prawn curry

SERVES 4

675 g/1½ lb uncooked large
  prawns or langoustines
  (scampi), weighed after
  removing heads and shells
4 tablespoons ghee
12 garlic cloves, thinly sliced
6–8 spring onions, chopped
½ red pepper, finely chopped
1–3 fresh red chillies, seeded
  and sliced
1 tablespoon tomato purée
3 tablespoons natural yogurt
2 tablespoons dried fenugreek
  (methi) leaves
225 g/8 oz rocket or watercress,
  chopped
2 tablespoons chopped fresh
  coriander leaves
2 teaspoons garam masala
salt

Spices

½ teaspoon each of cumin
  seeds, black mustard seeds,
  fennel seeds, green
  cardamom seeds
¼ teaspoon each of turmeric,
  chilli powder, mango powder,
  fenugreek seeds

Devein the prawns, rinse and pat dry.

Heat the ghee in a wok or karahi, then carry out the initial fry (page 36) with the spices, garlic and spring onions.

Add the pepper, chillies, tomato purée and yogurt. When they reach a gentle simmer, add the prawns and fenugreek leaves. Stir-fry until the prawns are cooked through; this will take about 6–8 minutes. Add a little water from time to time if necessary to keep the mixture moist.

Add the rocket or watercress, coriander leaves and garam masala and stir well. Add salt to taste, and serve at once.

For a change from rice or Indian bread, try this with oven - baked chips, dusted with chilli powder and garam masala.

LAHORI ACHARI ALOO
Potatoes in a pickle sauce

SERVES 4 AS A SIDE DISH

450g/1 lb small new potatoes
2 tablespoons vegetable oil
4 – 6 garlic cloves, very finely
    chopped
3 – 4 spring onions, finely
    chopped
1 tablespoon tomato purée
2 tablespoons natural yogurt
1 teaspoon chilli powder
4 tablespoons cooked peas
1 tablespoon fresh mint leaves
salt

Spices

1 teaspoon ground coriander
1 teaspoon ground cumin
1 teaspoon chilli powder
½ teaspoon mango powder
½ teaspoon garam masala
½ teaspoon turmeric

Boil the potatoes in their skins.

While they are cooking, heat the oil in a wok or karahi until hot but well below smoking point. Add all the spices and stir-fry briskly for about 30 seconds, then add the garlic and stir-fry for 3 – 4 minutes.

Add the spring onions, tomato purée, yogurt, chilli powder, peas, mint and salt to taste, then add the potatoes, and serve as soon as everything is mixed.

Serve hot or cold as a simple starter, accompanied by yogurt dip and chapatti. Follow with any curry, rice and vegetable dish. Alternatively, stuff inside naan bread for a snack meal.

MAHARANI DAL
The Queen's lentils

SERVES 4

225 g/8 oz black lentils (urid dal)
50 g/2 oz split red lentils
   (masoor dal)
4 tablespoons ghee
12 garlic cloves, finely chopped
2.5 cm/1 inch cube of fresh
   ginger, finely chopped
2 onions, finely chopped
50 ml/2 fl oz double cream
2 tablespoons chopped fresh
   coriander leaves
salt

Whole spices

2 teaspoons coriander seeds
1 teaspoon cumin seeds
2–3 brown cardamoms
2–3 pieces of cassia bark
3–4 bay leaves

Ground spices

1 teaspoon ground coriander
½ teaspoon ground cumin
½ teaspoon turmeric
½ teaspoon chilli powder
¼ teaspoon asafoetida
¼ teaspoon mango powder

Check the lentils and remove any grit or impurities. Rinse them several times, then soak in plenty of cold water for about 4 hours.

Drain and rinse the lentils, then measure an amount of water twice the volume of the drained lentils. Put the water in a 2.3 litre/4 pint saucepan and bring to the boil. Add the lentils and the whole spices and simmer for about 45 minutes, stirring occasionally, until the water is absorbed.

Meanwhile, heat the ghee in a wok or karahi and carry out the initial fry (page 36) with the ground spices, garlic, ginger and onion.

When the lentils have absorbed the water and are tender, add the stir-fried mixture, the cream, coriander and salt to taste. Mash lightly, then serve.

This dal accompanies any curry and rice combination, or makes a completely nutritious, filling meal simply with plain rice and some pickles.

NAVRATTAN PULLAO
Nine vegetables 'jewelled' rice

SERVES 4

4 tablespoons ghee
20–30 saffron strands
1 large onion, finely sliced
450 g/1 lb cooked rice
2 carrots, diced
¼ small red cabbage, diced
50 g/2 oz small green beans,
   diced
24 asparagus tips
3 tablespoons peas
3 tablespoons cooked sweetcorn
3 tablespoons cooked red kidney
   beans
3 tablespoons cooked chickpeas
6 radishes, quartered
2–3 tablespoons chopped fresh
   coriander leaves
salt

Spices
1½ teaspoons fennel seeds
3–4 green cardamoms, crushed
5–6 cloves, crushed
2–3 pieces of cassia bark
½ teaspoon black cumin seeds

Heat the ghee in a wok or karahi until hot, but well below smoking point. Add all the spices and stir-fry briskly for about 30 seconds. Add the saffron, stir briskly, then add the onion and mix well. Stir-fry briskly for a further 30 seconds. Keeping the heat high at first, stir-fry until the onion caramelizes; this will take 10–15 minutes and the heat should be lowered progressively during this time.

Meanwhile, reheat the rice and all the vegetables, ensuring they are all piping hot.

To serve, mix everything together, adding the fresh coriander and salt to taste. Serve at once.

This pillau is an ideal accompaniment to any curry, or it can be served as a meal in its own right. To make a spicy gravy to go with it, make a fragrant stock (page 37), which you should strain, then boil to reduce to a thicker consistency, adding some double cream and garam masala.

BARBUR'S BIRIANI
Meat with saffron rice

SERVES 4

225 g/8 oz basmati rice
6 tablespoons ghee or butter
5–6 garlic cloves, chopped
5 cm/2 inch cube of fresh ginger,
   finely chopped
2 onions, finely chopped
1–2 small fresh red chillies,
   shredded (optional)
450g/1 lb lean leg of lamb or
   beef, cubed
125 g/4 oz Greek-style yogurt
500 ml/16 fl oz fragrant stock
   (page 37)
25–30 saffron strands
3 tablespoons chopped fresh
   coriander leaves
2 teaspoons garam masala
   (page 37)
salt

Spices
4–5 green cardamoms
6–8 cloves
4–5 bay leaves
2–3 star anise pods
3–4 pieces of cassia bark
1½ teaspoons ground coriander
1 teaspoon ground cumin
1 teaspoon black peppercorns
½ teaspoon fennel seeds
½ teaspoon black cumin seeds
½ teaspoon turmeric

Preheat the oven to 190°C/375°F/Gas Mark 5. Rinse the rice, then soak for 10 minutes.

Heat 4 tablespoons of the ghee in a wok or karahi, then carry out the initial fry (page 36) with the spices, garlic, ginger, onion and chilli.

Add the meat and stir-fry for about 5–6 minutes to seal it. Add the yogurt and take the pan off the heat.

In a separate pan, bring the stock to the boil. Heat the remaining ghee in a lidded casserole dish of at least 3.4 litres/6 pints capacity. Drain the rice and add to the casserole, with the saffron. Stir until sizzling, then add the boiling stock. Put the lid on and leave the casserole over high heat for 3 minutes.

Stir in the meat mixture, then put the lid on the casserole and place in the oven.

After 25 minutes, gently (so as not to break the rice grains) fork around the biriani to aerate it and allow the steam to escape.

Add the coriander, garam masala and salt to taste. If the dish looks dry, add a little stock or water, then return it to the oven for a further 25 minutes.

Fork through the rice again, and test whether the meat is tender. It might need a further 10–20 minutes in the oven, so add more water if necessary. Serve hot.

This is a meal in itself – all you need are some curry condiments, such as a spicy gravy (see page 28), pickles, chutneys and Indian bread. Follow with fresh mango or mango sorbet.

AKBARI SHAHI TUKRI
Aromatic bread and butter pudding

SERVES 4

8 slices of white bread
vegetable oil for deep-frying
1 litre/1¾ pints milk
250 ml/8 fl oz sweetened
    condensed milk
½ teaspoon saffron strands
a few drops of vanilla essence
½ teaspoon ground green
    cardamom
a few drops of rosewater

Garnish
1 tablespoon flaked almonds,
    roasted
1 tablespoon pistachio nuts,
    chopped
4 silver or gold leaf sheets
    (optional, see page 35)

Preheat the oven to 190°C/375°F/Gas Mark 5.

Remove and discard the crusts from the bread. Heat the oil to 190°C/375°F or until a cube of bread browns in 30 seconds. Deep-fry the bread until golden, then drain on paper towels.

Using a non-stick saucepan to prevent burning, bring the milk to the boil, then reduce the heat to a simmer. Add the condensed milk and simmer for 15 minutes to thicken it, stirring occasionally. Add the saffron, vanilla essence, cardamom and rosewater, and remove from the heat.

Arrange four of the fried bread slices to cover the base of a small roasting tin. Place the other four slices on top. Pour the milk mixture over the bread, ensuring that the bread is thoroughly soaked.

Immediately place the tray in the oven and bake for 15 minutes. Serve hot or cold, garnished with the nuts and the silver or gold leaf.

Since this is quite a rich and filling pudding, I would serve it after a light curry such as the Chilli chicken (page 16) or the Fenugreek prawn curry (page 22).

The Basics

TECHNIQUES AND TIPS

Interchanging ingredients in curries is easy. For example, instead of lamb in the korma, duck in the pasanda or beef in the biriani, you may prefer an alternative meat, poultry, fish, shellfish or vegetables. You simply need to adjust the cooking times to about half or less if you use main ingredients other than meat.

PREPARING THE INGREDIENTS

Meat should be trimmed of veins, gristle and most fat, and should be cut into approximately 2.5 cm/1 inch cubes.

Poultry should be skinned and off the bone, and cut into approximately 4 cm/1½ inch cubes.

Fish should be gutted, cleaned and cut into 4 cm/ 1½ inch cubes. Prawns or scampi should be uncooked, shelled, deveined and washed.

Vegetables should be trimmed and washed, then cut into similar-sized pieces so that they take the same time to cook.

FREEZING

Meat, poultry, fish and shellfish curries freeze and reheat satisfactorily. Generally, vegetable curries do not.

GARNISHING

All curries benefit from a garnish that contrasts with the colour of the curry. The photographs give ideas, using toasted flaked almonds, pistachio nuts, desiccated coconut, red or green chilli strips, fresh coriander or mint leaves, chopped chives or spring onions, sprinklings of garam masala or paprika, swirls of cream or yogurt.

SERVING	Normally more than one curry is served, with rice and/or Indian bread. Side dishes of fruity chutneys, tangy pickles and mild raitas (yogurt sauces) can be added according to your taste.
SPECIALIST INGREDIENTS	Most of the spices used in these recipes are readily available at supermarkets and delicatessens. A few, though distinctive in the particular recipe, are harder to find and can be omitted. If you have difficulty obtaining specialist ingredients in the UK, write, enclosing a stamped, self-addressed envelope please, to: Pat Chapman, North Indian Curries, PO Box 7, Haslemere, Surrey GU27 1RP.
DRIED ONION FLAKES	These are available from supermarkets, and can sometimes be substituted for fresh onions, to save time and cooking smells.
EDIBLE GOLD OR SILVER LEAF (VARK)	The Moghul emperors used to garnish dishes such as korma, biriani and sweets with gold or silver leaf. Although it looks exotic, it is absolutely tasteless, but the Moghuls, it is said, believed it to be an aphrodisiac! Beware cheap imitations, which contain aluminium; the real thing is available by mail order, see above.

THE INITIAL FRY

To maximize flavours, curries require an initial stir-fry of the 'holy trinity' of spices, garlic and onion (sometimes a fourth is added – ginger). This 'initial fry' removes raw and bitter tastes from the spices, and as the garlic, ginger and onion turn golden brown, they caramelize (i.e. they become sweet in taste) and the ingredients become integrated. This 'initial fry' is the most important in the whole curry cooking process, and as it is used in many curry recipes in this book, I give it in detail here.

1 Heat the oil or ghee in a wok or karahi until hot, but well below smoking point.

2 If whole spices are being fried, add them to the oil or ghee and stir-fry briskly for about 30 seconds.

3 Add the garlic (and ginger, if specified) and continue to stir-fry briskly for a further 30 seconds.

4 Add the ground spices (if used), stir briskly, then add the onion and mix in well.

5 Keeping the heat high at first, stir-fry until the onion caramelizes. This will take between 10 and 15 minutes, depending on the degree of caramelization required. The heat will need to be lowered progressively during this time.

It saves considerable time, smells and washing up to make several batches of fried onion, with or without garlic and/or ginger. Divide what you make into portions and freeze in yogurt pots for future use.

Garam Masala

50 g/2 oz coriander seeds
50 g/2 oz cumin seeds
25 g/1 oz black peppercorns
2 or 3 pieces of cassia bark
2 teaspoons cloves
10 brown cardamoms
1 nutmeg
10 bay leaves
2 teaspoons ground ginger

Lightly roast everything except the ground ginger under a low to medium grill, or in a low oven (160°C/325°F/Gas Mark 3, for 5-10 minutes, until the spices are fragrant and give off a light steam – do not let them burn.

Leave to cool, then grind. You can use a coffee grinder if you grind only small quantities and break up large items first. Add the ground ginger, mix thoroughly and store in an airtight jar in a dark place. Garam masala will taste fresh for several months, but remember to make a fresh batch every few months to get the best flavours.

Fragrant stock

MAKES ABOUT 1 LITRE/1¾ PINTS

450 g/1 lb onions, coarsely
 chopped
10 garlic cloves, chopped
5 cm/2 inch cube of fresh
 ginger, chopped
2 or 3 large carrots, chopped
2 teaspoons salt

whole spices
10 cloves
10 green cardamoms
6 pieces of cassia bark
6 bay leaves

Bring 1.2 litres/2 pints water to the boil, then add all the ingredients. Simmer for 1 hour with the lid on, by which time the stock should have reduced by half. Strain and discard the solids.

If you like, add 225 g/8 oz meat trimmings and bones before you boil the stock.

Classic Cooking

STARTERS

Jean Christophe Novelli Chef/patron of Maison Novelli, which opened in London to great acclaim in 1996. He previously worked at the Four Seasons restaurant, London.

VEGETABLE SOUPS

Elisabeth Luard Cookery writer for the *Sunday Telegraph Magazine* and author of *European Peasant Food* and *European Festival Food*, which won a Glenfiddich Award.

GOURMET SALADS

Sonia Stevenson The first woman chef in the UK to be awarded a Michelin star, at the Horn of Plenty in Devon. Author of *The Magic of Saucery* and *Fresh Ways with Fish*.

FISH AND SHELLFISH

Gordon Ramsay Chef/proprietor of one of London's most popular restaurants, Aubergine, recently awarded its second Michelin star. He is the author of *A Passion for Flavour*.

CHICKEN, DUCK AND GAME

Nick Nairn Chef/patron of Braeval restaurant near Aberfoyle in Scotland, whose BBC-TV series *Wild Harvest* was last summer's most successful cookery series, accompanied by a book.

LIVERS, SWEETBREADS AND KIDNEYS

Simon Hopkinson Former chef/patron at London's Bibendum restaurant, columnist and author of *Roast Chicken and Other Stories* and the forthcoming *The Prawn Cocktail Years*.

VEGETARIAN

Rosamond Richardson Author of several vegetarian titles, including *The Great Green Gourmet* and *Food from Green Places*. She has also appeared on television.

PASTA

Joy Davies One of the creators of *BBC Good Food Magazine*, she has been food editor of *She, Woman* and *Options* and written for the *Guardian, Daily Telegraph* and *Harpers & Queen*.

CHEESE DISHES

Rose Elliot The UK's most successful vegetarian cookery writer and author of many books, including *Not Just a Load of Old Lentils* and *The Classic Vegetarian Cookbook*.

POTATO DISHES

Patrick McDonald Author of the forthcoming *Simply Good Food* and Harvey Nichols' food consultant.

BISTRO COOKING

Anne Willan Founder and director of La Varenne Cookery School in Burgundy and West Virginia. Author of many books and a specialist in French cuisine.

ITALIAN COOKING

Anna Del Conte is the author of *The Classic Food of Northern Italy* (chosen as the 1996 Guild of Food Writers Book of the Year) and *The Gastronomy of Italy*. She has appeared on BBC-TV's *Masterchef*.

VIETNAMESE COOKING
Nicole Routhier One of the United States' most popular cookery writers, her books include *Cooking Under Wraps*, *Nicole Routhier's Fruit Cookbook* and the award-winning *The Foods of Vietnam*.

MALAYSIAN COOKING
Jill Dupleix One of Australia's best known cookery writers, with columns in the *Sydney Morning Herald* and *Elle*. Author of *New Food*, *Allegro al dente* and the Master Chefs *Pacific*.

PEKING CUISINE
Helen Chen Learned to cook traditional Peking dishes from her mother, Joyce Chen, the grande dame of Chinese cooking in the United States. The author of *Chinese Home Cooking*.

STIR FRIES
Kay Fairfax Author of several books, including *100 Great Stir-fries*, *Homemade* and *The Australian Christmas Book*.

NOODLES
Terry Durack Australia's most widely read restaurant critic and co-editor of the *Sydney Morning Herald Good Food Guide*. He is the author of *YUM!*, a book of stories and recipes.

NORTH INDIAN CURRIES
Pat Chapman Started the Curry Club in 1982. Appears regularly on television and radio and is the author of eighteen books, the latest being *The Thai Restaurant Cookbook*.

BARBECUES AND GRILLS
Brian Turner Chef/patron of Turner's in Knightsbridge and one of Britain's most popular food broadcasters; he appears frequently on *Ready Steady Cook*, *Food and Drink* and many other television programmes.

SUMMER AND WINTER CASSEROLES
Anton Edelmann Maître Chef des Cuisines at the Savoy Hotel, London, and author of six books. He appears regularly on BBC-TV's *Masterchef*.

TRADITIONAL PUDDINGS
Tessa Bramley Chef/patron of the acclaimed Old Vicarage restaurant in Ridgeway, Derbyshire. Author of *The Instinctive Cook*, and a regular presenter on a new Channel 4 daytime series *Here's One I Made Earlier*.

DECORATED CAKES
Jane Asher Author of several cookery books and a novel. She has also appeared in her own television series, *Jane Asher's Christmas* (1995).

FAVOURITE CAKES
Mary Berry One of Britain's leading cookery writers, her numerous books include *Mary Berry's Ultimate Cake Book*. She has made many television and radio appearances and is a regular contributor to cookery magazines.

First published in 1997 by
George Weidenfeld & Nicolson
The Orion Publishing Group
Orion House
5 Upper St Martin's Lane
London WC2H 9EA

British Library Cataloguing-in-Publication data
A catalogue record for this book is available from the
British Library

ISBN 0 297 82280 2

Designed by Lucy Holmes
Edited by Maggie Ramsay
Food styling by Joy Davies
Typeset by Tiger Typeset